# THINKING INTO DESIRES

**Suryaprabha Easwar**

**FROM THOUGHT WE ARE MADE AND...
UNTO THOUGHT WE MUST SURRENDER**

Copyright © 2021 Suryaprabha Easwar

# Table of Contents

Acknowledgments .................................................................. ii

Introduction ........................................................................... 1

Chapter 1: Thought ................................................................ 3

Chapter 2: Paradigms ............................................................. 5

Chapter 3: Mental Faculties ................................................... 8

Chapter 4: Goals ................................................................... 11

Chapter 5: Awareness and Belief ......................................... 14

Chapter 6: Abundance .......................................................... 17

Chapter 7: Attitude ............................................................... 20

Chapter 8: Gratitude andAffirmation ................................... 23

Chapter 9: Laws of the Universe .......................................... 26

Chapter 10: Decision ............................................................ 30

Chapter 11: Serenity ............................................................. 34

Bibliography ......................................................................... 37

About The Author ................................................................ 38

# Acknowledgments

I always wanted to serve by writing. Creating an impact by writing is something that my soul demands. However, I never knew when and how I would start this journey till I found my mentors, Bob Procter and Mary Morrissey, who were highly instrumental in immensely transforming my life. I have gained deep insights about the laws of life that have motivated me to officially start studying these subjects in greater detail. Also, with their timeless masterpieces, great Authors such as Paulo Coelho and James Allen have always inspired me to keep studying and writing.

I must not forget my family - my parents, siblings, husband, daughter, colleagues, and friends for supporting me throughout the process, encouraging me to realize my dreams, and being around me always, no matter what, where, and when.

# Introduction

This pocketbook is a result of the study of Thoughts, their effects on life and well-being, and how by changing the thought, one can achieve the life of one's dreams. While the fundamental principles;the laws of nature aimed to be conveyed are not very different from what more experienced philosophers and scientists have already conveyed through their books and records, the author endeavors in each chapter of this book to provide simplified explanations withoutgetting too scientific to cater to readers from all walks of life. Each chapter has study notes, a related quote to inspire deep thinking, and an exercise to implement and test the contents.

This book intends to provide instant awareness to readers whenever a need arises or even a passive reading. Simply pull it out from your pocket, handbag, or mobile and read the chapter you like most! It is carefully curated into eleven brief chapters, with a very profound message and food for thought packed in each chapter. You will notice a logical progression of facts and motivational seeds in each chapter leading to a conclusive thought process that you can apply instantly anywhere, anytime.

It is recommended to keep this pocketbook or the e-version on your mobile phone always with you, wherever you go. The mere existence of the book with you will change the aura around you because of your altered state of mind by reading the chapters repeatedly as and when needed. The sole purpose of the book is to raise the reader's awareness level and flip the mind-set to a more creative and productive state.

# Chapter 1: Thought

What is a Thought? Thought is a form of energy, just like, heat and sound. It is a subtle element invisible to the eyes but is the force behind anything that later transforms into form. It is learned that Thought waves are cosmic waves that penetrate all time and space at once. Scientists say that Thought waves can travel within a fraction of a second, much faster than light or sound. They take formless energy and create a form – the image of what we are thinking about. Thoughts have frequency and can be measured by the level of awareness within us. It is an unlimited force.

Our thoughts affect our welfare and often affect others we think of. However, mere surface thoughts that are ordinary and trivial such as what we eat, wear, and shop, are not real thoughts. These are not called thinking at all. These are just mental activities. Thinking is when you focus on one theme or idea, latch on to it and go deep into it to achieve a certain result, i.e., conscious analysis of the information with a deep focus on Studying.

Therefore, focused and prolonged thought about an idea and understanding of the Truth, which arouses dormant powers, quickens the perceptions, and governs the life of man, would constitute Real Thinking. The thought energy flows to and through you; it has no form when it enters you. You give it direction, form, and emotion, resulting in that sequence of order. It is only with realthinking that one can change their life and achieve growth and success. This clearly means the kind of life you presently lead results from your current thought process.

What we deeply believe inside, which controls our aims, desires, and motives, constitute the real thought of an individual and is solely responsible for the course of our life and individual destiny. Therefore, it is important for us to train the mind to clear and exact thinking.

*The great 19th century Author James Allen wrote in his book As a Man Thinketh –*

*"Mind is the Master power that moulds and makes,*

*And Man is Mind, and evermore he takes the Tool of*

*Thought, and, shaping what he wills, brings forth a*

*thousand joys, a thousand ills: - He thinks in secret,*

*and it comes to pass: Environment is but his looking-*

*glass."*

Exercise: Spend two minutes consciously watching the thoughts that flow in your mind. Are you able to focus on one idea for more than 10 seconds?

# Chapter 2: Paradigms

From Chapter 1, we have understood that our life depends on what we think. Therefore, if you need to change your life, you must change your thinking! Know that Results are caused by Actions, Actions are sourced from Habits, and Habits are sourced from beliefs. And Beliefs are sourced from Paradigms. It all starts with the Paradigms. A paradigm is a set of ideas; it is a way of looking at something. When you change paradigms, you're changing how you think about something and, therefore, the results.

But paradigms are not built in a day. They get into man, even before he is conceived through their parents' DNA, then through the journey inside the mother's womb, from the environment during growth and nurturing, school, friends, relatives, and later through news, TV, social media, books, and so on. If you are made to believe that you cannot fly or you must not try to fly, you will never even try. A hundred years ago, no one would have believed that we could have FaceTime on a handheld phone across the world. But we do this all the time now!

Great men such as the Wright Brothers (for the first airplanes) and Thomas Alva Edison (for the first incandescent light bulbs) have changed and challenged the general thought process, getting new results that have transformed the world. To change the thought, therefore, they must have reprogrammed their thinking and altered their paradigms by replacing them with new beliefs not known to mankind earlier. How did they do it? They built a new model. They replaced the old paradigms, not only in their minds but in the minds of millions of fellow humans around the world. You must know that, just like hundreds of computer terminals connected to the main server, each of our minds is like a terminal connected to the larger Universal Intelligence through the subconscious mind. Each computer has its own set of programs (paradigms).

There are only two known ways to change the paradigm. The constant spaced repetition of ideas, which are essentially opposite to paradigms and the personal experience of an Emotional Impact. You can change paradigms by pressing certain idea(s) repeatedly into the subjective mind (subconscious), which alters the emotional state in your body leading to actions that produce results in the desired way. Emotions are applications that connect the programs to the main server (the universal intelligence stated above). By placing the new idea in the heart (emotional mind), you are opening a free flow of two-way communication between inner intellect and the Universal Intelligence, moving up to a new higher frequency where all circumstances needed to achieve your goals will move towards manifesting that idea.

*Einstein said, "Everything is energy and that's all there is to it. Match the frequency of the reality you want, and you cannot help but get that reality. It can be no other way. This is not philosophy, this is physics."*

Exercise: Think of something new that you have never thought of before! Try focusing on it and think about it repeatedly several times a day. Suddenly, a rush of new knowledge and information will start flowing in towards you about this idea from all directions.

# Chapter 3: Mental Faculties

From Chapter 2, we understood that to change paradigms; we need a shifting of thoughts. But every time you have a new idea, you must put up with another strong conflicting voice inside you – let's call it what if? And then the idea is given up in a few minutes, weeks, or days. Again, you hit upon an idea, and once again, the voice says, 'What if it turns out not as I expect? What if something bad happens?' and thus, the idea is lost to fear. The conflict goes on and on. So, you are stuck with the same result year after year, frustrated and miserable.

One must realize that human beings are the highest form of creation, and we are gifted with six beautiful jewels which we can use to grow and prosper. Unlike other creatures, we can create our own environment with these six faculties. These are Perception, Will, Memory, Imagination, Reason, and Intuition. How much effort do you really put into developing one or more of these faculties? Deep research and several years of study in any field, such as arts, physics, and mathematics, would have created a genius like Einstein. Let us elaborate on these faculties a little bit.

- *<u>Perception</u> is the ability to look or feel something* *differently*

- *Will is the ability to make a strong decision no matter what happens*

- *Memory is the ability to preserve and recover information*

- *Imagination is the ability to create anything within the mind.*

- *Reasoning is the understanding of cause and effect - logical thinking*

- *Intuition is the ability to connect to the language of spirit without conscious reasoning - the Universal Intelligence – the substance from which all things were formed on earth*

Use these mental faculties to create the world you want for yourself and your family to live in. Never Settle. Even though you understand these by reading or listening, it's only 'You' who can work on changing the way you think; no one else can do this for you. This explains why there are millions of men and women having superior knowledge and high education level, still living in poor conditions with inferior results. One must ask themselves then, "What do I want? Fix the thought on the 'want' and study it in detail using these valuable faculties." If you have a desire inside you, you can make it your reality. You just need to know what steps to take to make it happen, which we shall discuss in the upcoming chapter.

*Einstein said: "The intuitive mind is a sacred gift and the rational mind is a faithful servant. We have created a society that honors the servant and has forgotten the gift."*

<u>Exercise:</u> Take a problematic situation in your life today; write it down on a piece of paper and put it at the center of a table. Review to see how this will be resolved by becoming different people who inspire you, every time sitting on a different side of the table. You will be amazed at the number of different ways this can be solved. In this exercise, you have nearly used all your faculties. You can do this exercise repeatedly, many times throughout your lifetime, for adifferent problem each time!

# Chapter 4: Goals

A rose plant has but one goal: grow, expand, and produce roses nurtured by sunlight and water. Every other creature has its own goal, too, to expand and breed. Humans, on the other hand, have been gifted with mental faculties mentioned in previous chapters but do not come pre-packaged with specific goals. Why? It is because <u>WE can create our own environment</u>, our own goals, and find our own purpose in life. We are here to create our world like the original Omnipotent God created us from his Thoughts.

<u>When something is created with speed and accuracy, it becomes an Efficient Production.</u> Efficient production gives positive results. For this, the mental faculties need to be trained in a step-by-step orderly process. Each step then becomes a Goal to achieve in life's journey.

When you decide to travel to a certain country, you give clear destination details to the booking agent for booking the ticket. When you need to go to a certain movie, you book a ticket for the right title, time, date, and location. Have you ever wondered what is your life's destination and purpose and built a vision around it? Vision is the big picture of 'What' you want in life, the purpose is the reason or 'Why' you are here, and the goal is the 'How' to achieve it. Each goal is a step toward achieving the larger Vision. So, goals will be short-term and keep changing until you attain the bigger Vision. Each goal, when accomplished, provides further motivation and inspiration for the next higher level. Goals need to be nurtured by creating favorable conditions like positive emotions and motivation. You may struggle with getting a promotion in your day job, or your art passion is not giving you the desired income; you want recognition, an award, a relationship, a family, or a dog! Whatever it may be. Set a goal, work on upskilling your faculty, and focus on the goal with your thought energy. As a result, the 'How' will magically unfold itself!

In large corporations, Goal setting and assessment is part of the annual employee performance review exercise. How do we set a goal, then? A goal should be something you can see clearly, but your current situation, circumstance, beliefs, and resources do not permit you to attain it easily. It can be anything – starting a business, learning to paint, a senior corporate position, writing a book, anything that you have not done before, or anything that you want to do much bigger. It should not be something that you already know how to do or how to achieve. The frequency of the new goal should be at a much higher level than the frequency on which your current results sit. Set a goal that really excites you, something that will eventually expand you. Wallace D. Wattles, the great American New Age Thoughts Writer, said:

*You must begin to do what you can do where you are, and you must do all that you can where you are. You can advance only by being **larger than** your present place.*

Exercise: Think of an idea, target, or goal which is well above what you already know how to achieve. Set an approximate date of fruition. Write it down on a small card and carry it with you all the time to feel its vibration continuously. Consciously focus your actions towards achieving this every day. The process will repeat until it is achieved and then a new, more exciting goal should be set.

# Chapter 5: Awareness and Belief

In the previous exercise, we saw that setting a goal holding on to a vision willfully creates an opening in the mind to receive more information towards achieving the goal, thereby placing you in a new level of awareness. A painter paints better, an athlete runs faster, a movie becomes a super hit, and so on. Thus, setting a goal and expecting to see the result in a certain way puts you on a higher frequency level where people, things, and services that support the goal are now moving towards you, contributing to the fruition of your goal. Thus, we can say:

*Awareness is the ability to connect to the universal spirit or power on a certain frequency. Belief is the expectation of the outcome that will be manifested.*

There are infinite levels of frequencies, all connected to one above and one below. Access to universal knowledge is freely and fairly available to one and all. As we move our goals higher, our awareness levels will increase simultaneously. To simplify this, these have been described as seven levels, lowest to highest:

- <u>Animal</u> – React, Fight, or Flight; living with basic instincts only.

- <u>Mass</u> – Doing what everyone else does getting up, going to work, having lunch at noon, and so on.
- <u>Aspiration</u> – Desiring something greater than the masses.
- <u>Individual</u> – Expressing your uniqueness.
- <u>Discipline</u> – Giving yourself a command and following it.
- <u>Experience</u> – Seeing how action changes your results.
- <u>Mastery</u> – Respond, think, and plan.

The journey from Reaction to Response – these states of Awareness may be reached by anyone through years of focused study and experience. Mystery is only another name for ignorance; all things are mysterious when they are not adequately understood. Mere awareness of information, without expecting the desired result, is like writing a code with no execution button. Belief is when you are aware of your winning even before you run the race. In other words, you must believe in your desire as if it is already yours to be able to manifest it. By doing this, you are exercising the faculty of 'Will' on your want and holding the vision steadfastly to move into the positive emotional state, which causes vibration in the body that puts you in a new frequency of reception. Whereas fear is a state where you are unsure of the outcome due to external factors or your own paradigms. Fear has the same effect on results as belief has because both are backed by emotions (execution buttons connecting to God'sCloud), one on a higher frequency level and the other lower.

*Andrew Carnegie, one of the richest American Industrialists of the 18th century, said: "Any idea that is held in the mind, that is emphasized, that is either <u>feared</u> or <u>revered</u>, will begin at once to cloth itself in the most convenient and appropriate form available."*

<u>Exercise:</u> Take a sheet of paper and on the left-hand side, write down three paradigms you believe are stopping your progress, and on theright half, write down three paradigms that have helped you succeed in life. Then tear the left half of the page and burn it (safely) into ashes, consciously feeling the emotion of these negatives leaving you for good.

# Chapter 6: Abundance

Abundance is the availability of things more than its demand. When something is available in excess, it is called abundance. Let's say the air we breathe is abundant. It contains more oxygen than we need to live. The Lord God has created an abundance of everything on this earth. When we speak of abundance and riches, people tend to think of money. Let us get this clear first; that Money is the unit with which we can measure the current financial state or growth –measure our results - it's nothing more than that. Money is limited in quantity; within the government, the state, and the nation. But what is not limited is the ability to provide things and services for that money. The ideas that man can think of are unlimited- as thereis no limit to imagination. If one can hold on to an idea, work steadfastly with will and discipline and get results to provide valuable service to the larger society, he can earn money in abundance. That is what abundance means in spirit. When we can think of more abundance, we shall receive more abundantly. Thus, the level of abundance in one's life, one's financial income, health,and well-being, is dependent on three driving factors that govern the Natural Laws, which will be detailed in a later chapter.

You cannot expect something for nothing. It is the reward of what work you do; in fact, the reward of your thoughts. We can say that it's a state of vibration then because we have already seen in earlier chapters that thoughts create vibrations that produce your current results. The bigger your idea, the more valuable and unique it is, and the larger its scope of service, the financial yield will be higher. In other words, for you to be in a state of receiving abundance, you must be in a state of giving abundance.

What is life giving you today? Health, happiness, and abundance, or sickness, misery, and lack? Whatever it is, it is your own as you have created it. It belongs to no one else but you. You make your own investments, and you are enjoying the profits or losses daily. If you are unhappy with your investments, it may be wise for you to note what you invested in, review it, and make changes needed to manifest abundance in your life. Only your own can come to you, and all that is yours will surely come to you. But there is no limit to how much you can take from the spirit because there is no limit to ideas and imagination; there is no limit to where thoughts can take you. No one can control your thoughts and actions, which continually progress towards manifesting all the good that you want. Pay attention to your input and imagination to be able to live an abundant life. Therefore we say, 'there is already abundance everywhere; only man has to learn and see better'. Neville Goddard, the great American Author of Mysticism, said:

*We are only limited by weakness of attention and poverty of imagination.*

Exercise: Pick up an aspect in life where you do not feel abundant, e.g., employment income. Review how you can improve your current contribution to make it more valuable and increase the scope of your service and its quality. New ideas will start flowing to you, which, when put into action, sooner or later, will yield results much more than you expect.

# Chapter 7: Attitude

From the previous chapter, we understood that the spirit, universal intelligence has no limits and provides an abundance of good to all beings equally. How can one explain so many of disparities in the world, then? (combine below para with this). It is through wealth, health, employment, business etc. Two businessmen selling the same service in the same locality may be getting different results. Certain sections of some nations are extremely poor up to several generations and live on world charities. This means there must be something in our <u>ability to receive</u> good that is the cause of such disparities.

The best way to explain this is using a financial situation. Let's say you have only $180 in the bank account with which you need to paya mortgage of $300 and a child's school fee of $80, which together exceeds your account balance, and there is no other income till the end of the month. How can you not worry and fret? *The trick is* ***youdon't deny the fact that you have only $180, but you deny the power of the fact that you have only $180 to control your life.*** You must then alter your fear or worry into thinking, '*The amount is what is in my account, but I am an abundant being and part of an abundance universe*'. Get into a vibration of abundance even though facts are what they are. An idea will come to you, bringing new income with it. This is what Attitude is all about.

Our predominant mental attitude is the primary cause of most things that come into our lives. The positive affirmation will emotionally move into a frequency where ideas will start coming to you. Idea is God's currency, which is unlimited, while Money is man's currency and may be limited. One must live inside out and not outside in. The amount of money in your account does not dictate your state of mind; the inner affirmation dictates your state and changes your results from the outside. When you internalize the goal, you turn it into infinite intelligence, the power of the spirit that flows to and through you.

Over time, you develop the mastery of manifesting thoughts into a form from the inside out. Be aware that all our problems are mental in nature, and they have no existence outside of us. One's state in life is largely determined by one's mental attitude. Some people radiate discouragement, gloom, and failure because they accept an 'I can't' attitude. Others positively emanate success through a cheerful, confident, energetic 'I can' attitude. The former category gravitates to conditions of adversity, ill luck, and misfortune, while the latter attracts the very best and rises on and on to success. Your attitude is a sum of your thoughts, feelings, and actions. Therefore, they can be either positive or negative. The only way you can improve the results you are getting in life is to take full responsibility for your Attitude. A new attitude is required for better wealth, health, lifestyle, relationships etc.

*The great American philosopher and historian William James said: The greatest discovery of my generation is that human beings can alter their lives by altering their attitudes of mind.*

<u>Exercise:</u> Attitudes can change only by repeated affirmations which have to face the conflict from deep-rooted paradigms. You may make repeated affirmation statements such as "I am very powerful and successful, or I am abundant" by writing it down in a notebook fifty times as often as possible. Remember the paradigm from Chapter 2? It is hard to change it. But you can change it with repeated affirmations.

# Chapter 8: Gratitude and Affirmation

Personal Development Coaches and consultants have for a long time emphasized that Affirmations and Gratitude must be practiced as often as possible to be able to receive all goodness in life continuously. Let us analyze the relationship between these two because unless one understands fully, there will be some level of embarrassment to practice anything just because one is told to do. For example, you will be quite embarrassed to make a positive affirmative statement looking at the mirror or writing a journal everyday with affirmation statements, to begin with. Let us understand that when we '*Thank*' someone for something, we acknowledge the receipt of something good. This acknowledgmentputs the receiver and the giver amidst a positive vibration; the receiver feels abundant, and the giver feels rewarded and appreciated for the task performed. This positive vibration helps both to stay within the realms of a positive frequency. Expressing displeasure over anything will trigger emotions of fear and sadness which does the opposite, moving us away from the set goal, which sits at a much higher frequency than the current result. Remember, we said that the goal should be set at a much higher level than current results. Therefore, the longer and more frequent one stays in the positive vibration, the easier it becomes to achieve the goal. Gratitude is a tool that will lead your mind out along the ways things come to you.

But affirmations and gratitude statements may not be an embarrassing practice at all. It will be surprising to note that such practices are already built into our society and culture, no matter which part of the world you are from. You may use the opportunities of everyday activities to make these powerful statements instead of allocating a set time for the affirmation. An easier approach to gratitude would be as follows:

Consciously add emotion into our daily actions, big or small, by feeling thankful for receiving or getting rewarded for tasks completed. Keep doing this until it becomes a spontaneous habit built into your lifestyle. This includes appreciating and thanking your own self for a job well done, even if it's a baby step toward the set goal. The self-appreciation should include statements that you have already achieved the desired goal to keep you on a higher frequency level than where the desired goal exists. Besides, buy yourself a small gift, which is even more rewarding.

Prayers are also meant to be gratitude statements; however, the requests must be made from the heart rather than from the lips alone. Continuous practice of conscious Gratitude and Affirmation gradually changes your whole outlook toward life. But, practice generating emotion along with gratitude, directing where you recognize the good, even in the face of adversity, and soon you will find the adversity disappearing. The magic lamp of spirit will show up to you. When we fail to acknowledge, we cut the wire from God of receiving the greater good. Remember, Faith is born out of Gratitude. *My Mentor and Coach, Bob Proctor, says:*

*'Learn to give willingly and receive graciously.'*

Exercise: When you say thank you to anyone for anything, pause, look into the eyes, smile, and say it with emotion. For every action step towards achieving your set goal, no matter how small it is, appreciate yourself, stating, "I am so happy and grateful that I have now…"

# Chapter 9: Laws of the Universe

When God – the Original Energy, Source, or Formal Substance created us, the patterns and plots were first formed in His mind by thought energy. Then the idea materialized into forms, rules were written down, and an orderly sequence was followed. Laws were made. Whatever has been achieved in life, the natural laws have been followed in an orderly fashion, even without our knowledge.

<u>*Since we are part of the same original energy, by the same law, we can achieve anything by imagining a thing, holding it in mind, and feeding it with emotion which then causes vibrations in the body to take actions that produce results*</u>. Forms can be changed by changing the vibration of molecules in it, like water changes to steam or ice by heating or cooling. Similarly, you can convert an idea in your mind into a visible result, such as a bank account, car, house, job, health, well-being, etc., by moving into the required level of vibration. Therefore, you can get what you want not by doing certain things but by doing things in a certain way, as the Natural Law requires you to. The best definition of Natural Law seems to be the uniform and orderly method of the omnipotent God. Therefore, it is our basic duty to

provide the right environment for our intellectual seeds to achieve what we want. Let us briefly define each of these laws:

*The Law of Perpetual Transmutation* – Thought energy, when held in mind most often, will materialize into results that you see in your life. It is, therefore, essential to focus on productive and developmental thoughts.

*The Law of Relativity* – Nothing is good or bad, big or small until you *relate* it to something. When you relate your situation to something much worse than you, you always feel good.

*The Law of Vibration* – Everything, including us, is a mass of energy vibrating at high speed. Nothing rests. Conscious awareness of this vibration is called *feeling*. When you are not feeling good, think seriously about something you should be grateful for to change your vibration.

*The Law of Polarity* – Everything has an opposite: hot–cold, up – down, etc. When you acknowledge the good, you move to that vibration and attract better.

*The Law of Rhythm* – The tide goes in and out, nights fade into days, and there are good and bad times. Awareness of this will help you sail through bad times easily with faith and hold on to faith with strength.

*The Law of Cause and Effect* – Whatever you send to the universe comes back. It is scientifically proven that Actions and Reactions are equal and opposite. Concentrate on what and how much good you can do; do not worry about what you will get, and the law will take care of the rest.

*The Law of Gender* – Each seed has a gestation and incubation period. Similarly, ideas are spiritual seeds and will take their time to move into physical results. Your goals will manifest in their own time. Know they will.

Lord helps those who help themselves, meaning the law helps those who work harmoniously with it. We become what we think about. All we need to focus on is to work with the laws. *Dr. Warner Von Braun, the father of the US space program, said:*

*"The natural laws of the universe are so precise that we do not have any difficulty building a spaceship, sending a person to the moon, and we can time the landing with the precision of a fraction of a second."*

*As Wallace Wattles points out,*

*"You can act in accordance with these laws, or you can disregard them, but you can in no way alter them. The laws forever operate and hold you to strict accountability, and there is not the slightest allowance for ignorance… Once a person learns and*

*obeys these laws, he will get rich with mathematical certainty."*

Exercise: Think of at least 5 things you have already accomplished in your life and relate them to the above-mentioned Laws of the Universe to connect the dots and realize how they would have worked in your favor. Write them down in a journal. Equipped with this new awareness and belief, it will now become a lot easier for you to set and accomplish newer goals more efficiently and effortlessly.

*Let me quote a paragraph from Page 25 of the book Wings of Fire by Dr.APJ Abdul Kalam:*

*"Desire, when it stems from the heart and spirit when it is pure and intense, possesses awesome electromagnetic energy. This energy is released into the ether each night as the mind falls into the sleep state. Each morning it returns to the conscious state reinforced with the cosmic currents. That which has been imaged will surely and certainly be manifested. You can rely, young man, upon this ageless promise as surely as you can rely upon the eternally unbroken promise of sunrise... and the Spring."*

# Chapter 10: Decision

We have seen so far that by changing thoughts and acting in line with the laws of the Universe, it's possible to change the results in our life. However, here is something that is critical to sustained growth and development - DECISION - this is a very strong attribute to great leaders, and the good news is that it is something that can be developed by practice over time. Since Success is a progressive realization of a worthy ideal *(as defined by Earl Nightingale),* hence we need a Decision tool that will be able to help us pour in continuous focus.

The Oxford Dictionary defines 'Decision' as a conclusion or resolution reached after consideration. That means, after thinking of a desired result using will and reasoning; you have made a commitment to yourself that you agree to a certain action or resolution. Mark the work COMMITMENT. This is where the KEY lies - Decision is the opposite of procrastination. Decision, or the lack of it, is responsible for the breaking or making of many careers.

More often than not, we make a decision to do or be something and then get stuck in a dilemma – Do it – don't do it, Say it – don't say it, Go there – don't go there, Leave it – don't leave it. The loop of emotional war – also called ambivalence – the co-existence of two opposite feelings towards the same objective, and this is very damaging to both the mind and the body. And then continuous progress remains a dream forever. It happens to everyone many times throughout their lifetime.

As Dr. Carole N Hildebrand rightly points out – "There is a corollaryelement that must go hand in hand with the decision... and that is *commitment*." For example, if you have decided to buy a house but are not committed to it, it is no decision. It's just a wish.

So, start making REAL Decisions!! And for this, you need courage. Here is a three-point step to make the decision-making process easy for you. You can virtually eliminate conflict and confusion and bring in a clear pattern of living only by becoming proficient in making decisions. Let's say making a decision is simply answering a set of questions that will eliminatate any ambivalence in the first place, the only condition being, 'You' must do it for and by yourself.

-Will doing, being, or having this move me in the direction of my Goal?

-Does doing, being, or having this go in harmony with the laws of the Universe?

-Will doing, being, or having this violate the rights of

others?

-If the answer to the first two questions is yes and the last question is no, fearlessly make the committed decision. Do not go about asking others: '*What do you think?*' If it's your life, go ahead and make your own decision. This Decision, a single mental move you can make, will, in a millisecond, solve enormous problems for you.

One of the main causes of indecision is a person's firm belief in limited supply. As you are now aware of abundance and supply, you will realize there is never any limit, and you have potentially unlimited resources around you. With this knowledge and process explained above, you will be able to make Real Committed Decisions going forward to live the life of your dreams. Decision is a subject every parent should teach their children at a very young age, not by making decisions for them but by allowing them to make their own decisions. James Allen – "*We think in secret, and it comes to pass. The environment is but a looking glass.*" This translates to the idea that no one can see you making decisions, but they will almost always see the results of your decisions.

"*Go as far as you can see. When you get there… you will see how to go further.*" Carlyle. <u>Exercise:</u> Pick up one area where you are in a state of ambivalence now, and make a clear decision using the above three-point process; take the burden of procrastination, and the next steps will automatically show up.

*Also, please read Sequel 2 of this personal development series – *Thinking into Success*

# Chapter 11: Serenity

You have seen how, by conscious efforts, you can move towards your set goal. As you move toward your goal, it moves toward you. However, calmness of mind is important to be in the state of creating.

When a person is worried or stressed, asking him to practice breathing exercises or focus on candle light may really not be helpful. What can be done, however, is to focus on one goal or priority with increased attention resulting in productivity, which in turn will motivate and prepare the person for the next bigger goal. This goal has risen from his desire and therefore is not a burden to his soul. This comes through practice.

In 'Serenity', the last chapter in the book *As a Man Thinketh*, James Allen wrote:

*"Calmness of Mind is one of the beautiful jewels of wisdom. It is the result of long and patient effort in self-control. Its presence is an indication of ripened experience and of a more than ordinary knowledge of the laws and operations of thought."*

When your level of awareness increases, as seen in the Chapter on Awareness, you move gradually from a Reactive state to a Responsive state and finally attain Mastery. As per the Laws of theUniverse, by knowing how to govern yourself, by applying these principles, and by knowing and practicing a *certain way of life*, your worry and fear will gradually disappear, which in turn will revere spiritual strength. As you now know, with mastery, all around you will gradually know that they can learn from you and rely upon you. The more tranquil you become, the greater the success, the influence, and the power of good. There can be no greater example of this than the great Indian Non-Violent Freedom Fighter Mahatma Gandhi. 'The great words of *Mahatma Gandhi* are worth noting:*" Be the change you want to see..."*

Meditation is believed to be a tool to practice calmness of mind. However, as much as it is being hyped and marketed and minted into money, it is my strong personal belief that Calmness of Mind can be built into our daily routines by practicing altered thinking which dispels fear or worry through deep faith. Quoting the profound words by Sir James Allen:

*"Tempest-tossed souls, wherever ye may be, under whatsoeverconditions ye may live, know this in the ocean of life the isles of Blessedness are smiling, and the sunny shore of your ideas awaits your coming. Keep your hand firmly upon the helm of thought. In the bank of your soul reclines the commanding Master; He does but sleep: wake Him, Self-control is strength; Right Thought is Master; Calmness is Power. Say unto your heart, "Peace, be still!"*

<u>Exercise:</u> The best way to practice a calm mind is simply consciously telling yourself to actually 'Calm Down' and focus on the one thing at hand. Make a priority list and complete them in that order, appreciating yourself for every task completed. This will be far more fruitful and effortless than cluttering and multitasking several things, resulting in poor productivity.

# Bibliography

1. Doctor A.P.J Abdul Kalam and Arun, Tiwari (1999), Biography Title: Wings of Fire, India

2. Allen, James (1903) Book Title: As a Man Thinketh, England

3. Bob Proctor (2021) Seminar Workbook Titled Science of Getting Rich based on the book Science of Getting Rich by Wallace D Wattles, Arizona, US.

4. Bob Proctor & Mary Morrissey (2021) Seminar Workbook Titled Working with the Law based on teachings by Dr. Raymon Holliwell (1964)

5. Bob Proctor (2018) - Proctor Gallagher Institute Materials Tiled The Nature of Vibration.

6. Availableat:https:www.proctorgallagherinstitute.com/28977/the nature-of- vibration

7. Albert Einstein Quotes:https:quoteinvestigator.com/2013/09/18/intuitive-mind

8. Andrew Carnegie https:jimdiaferio.wordpress.com/2011/07/09/Andrew carnegie-quote/

9. Wattle, D Wallace & Dr. Warner Von Braun Quote:https://30lawsofflow.com/universal-laws-2/
   9.Dr. Carole N Hildrebrand's on Decision

10. 2004 - Life Success Production – Â https://www.freedomeducation.ca/ free-report/Decision.pdf

# About The Author

Suryaprabha Easwar is a Award winning Dubai based Author, Coach and Researcher on the Laws of Life, dedicated to sharing her life-transformative insights worldwide through mentoring programs, public speeches, and writing. Her motto is to raise public awareness about the concept of living *Inside Out,* exploring the fullest inner potential, which is the secret of true bliss and success, and making life more meaningful and worthy for the seekers!

**Contact the Author: suryaprabhae@gmail.com**

# THINKING
## INTO
# DESIRES

In a world where thoughts hold the power to shape reality, "Thinking into Desires" unveils an extraordinary journey through the uncharted territories of the mind - enlightening the readers about the possibility of changing the course of life, achieving desired objectives, and sustainable success by changing the way one THINKS. Using the natural gifts of mental faculties such as imagination, perception, and will the book convinces the readers that thoughts materialize into tangible manifestations, and with the application of the principles of the Laws of the Universe one can find themself in a reality where the line between imagination and existence blurs - the dimensions of space and time collapse with awareness and practice of these principles.

www.ingramcontent.com/pod-product-compliance
Lightning Source LLC
Chambersburg PA
CBHW052107110526
44591CB00013B/2385